A Primer
on the Right

*The challenge of the modern Right
and how it relates to the contemporary Left*

Robert E. Salyer

TABLE OF CONTENTS

INTRODUCTION

From the fall of Soviet Communism down to 2016, Liberalism represented the default language of political discourse in the Western world.[1] Probably most people in Europe and practically all in America believed that the entire political spectrum spoke this common language, underlined by universal political values such as pluralism and liberal democracy, liberal capitalism, secularism, equality, and an explicit commitment to human rights.

During this (interregnum?) period, the political Left (understood as progressive Liberalism, social democracy, and including various forms of non-revolutionary Socialism) worked steadily to translate most of these

---

1 In 2006 Francis Fukuyama famously published *The End of History and the Last Man*, expressing an opinion held by many in the West that they lived in the age of the final triumph of liberal democracy and capitalism.

universal political values into legal, economic, and social realities. Given the practical universality of these values, the Left's engagement with the Right of the time (understood as classical Liberalism, and having a greater focus on liberal capitalism) concentrated mainly on demonstrating to the Right that the latter was merely in error as to the ramifications of the shared liberal worldview. In the Left's view, the accepted Right—*e.g.*, the pre-Trump Republican Party in the United States—existed only as a foil, slowing change, ensuring the process did not jar the socio-economic system too abruptly. Thus, the operational goals of Center-Left political parties—*e.g.*, Tony Blair's Labour Party in Britain—could focus on expanding the reach of the welfare state, social democracy, and the mores of an inclusive, open society; while the Center-Right political parties would mount, at best, prudential challenges to most of these programs, even while seeking to safeguard the ostensibly free market economy. The Right pre-2016 provided no substantive, principled challenge to the Liberal project, and was in fact from a certain perspective, intrinsically vital to this project. Save certain seemingly anachronistic public figures (all of whom could safely be ignored), *e.g.*, a Patrick Buchanan in the United States, or a Jean-Marie le Pen in France, no one acknowledged the existence of moral disagreement.

As of 2016, moral disagreement has broken out. A "new" Right has seemingly emerged to displace the old.[2] The recently liberated peoples of Eastern Europe have arisen as a sea of nationalist-populist resistance to perceived Western "decadence" and deracination, as political events in Hungary and Poland have borne out. President Vladimir Putin of Russia openly abuses "obsolete" liberal democracy, and he has in essence assumed the role of autocratic steward for the Russian Orthodox Church. The United Kingdom has arguably stepped away in spirit from ever-increasing global integration,

---

2 It is of course arguable just how new this "new" Right really is. It may be more accurate to say that, after years of post-war consensus in the noncommunist world favoring some form of Liberalism, authentic and unabashed Right-wing attitudes have re-emerged.

opting instead in 2016 to withdraw from the European Union. Perhaps most conspicuously of all, the United States of America in 2016 elected a leader in President Donald Trump, who views globalism and its accompanying humanist internationalism with at least some suspicion if not downright hostility.

This new non-Liberal Right has been less than forthcoming in identifying the fundamentals of its moral disagreement with the Left, leaving both sides perplexed. This lack of clarity as to the nature of the disagreement is due in large part to the fact that this new Right is populist-driven, and seems relatively ignorant of itself. The Right tends to "feel" its principles, rather than consciously articulate them. Thus, tangible principles of the Right are still largely a mystery, not only for the Left, but also for the Right itself.

This stems to some degree from the fact that the Left and Right are not analogues. The Left's political project aims implicitly, and sometimes explicitly, at an ideal polity, *i.e.*, an abstract utopia. This utopia, simply put, would define itself as the prosperous society of self-actualizing individuals.

In contrast, the Right does not have a political project, at least not an abstract one. Rather, its political engagement usually begins from premises assumed unconsciously, as noted, and it proceeds immediately thereafter to operate according to the Liberal language of discourse, the only language it has known for some time. This language cannot serve the Right in the long run however, because it is a language grounded in part upon a critique of value preference. Yet, value preferences are at the heart of the Right's premises. The shared Liberal language ends up logically undermining these premises, and translating them into mere subjective dross. Thus, the new Right has inevitably found itself hamstrung in defending itself. On the other hand, the Left has often times found itself incapable of grasping the sources of conflict with its opponent.

A succinct meta-analysis of how the Left and Right differ, might describe the latter as engaging in definite "preferences," all stemming from how the Right evaluates the world around it. In rebuttal, the Left critiques and rejects the Right's evaluations as unfounded, and proposes what the world would look like if the illegitimate evaluations were removed. However, such a description of the Left and Right would be so abstruse, as well as unsubstantial, as to be next to useless. More meat is required.

This work aspires to shed some light on Rightist first principles, and implications therefrom. It does not propose to argue against them, nor does it propose to explain them away. Certainly however, the failure to articulate the principles and premises underlying the actual positions and substantive attitudes of the Right has had negative consequences for it. While the failure in articulation encourages the perception by its Leftist critics that today's Right is merely reactive and aimless, defined only in opposition (often visceral), or at best anchored in fleeting (and sometimes bombastic) assertions, within the Right's large sympathetic populist base this failure in articulation actually helps to make the perception a reality. The Right largely does not seem to know itself. What does it truly mean to be on the Right?

The predilections (as opposed to principles or positions) of the political Right in the Western world, and of Conservatism generally, are of course widely recognized. They include an instinctual impetus to conserve prescriptions from the past, both economic and social. They include certain historical beliefs, and they usually include an endorsement of the importance of Western Civilization.

This short primer attempts to broadly corral principles and evaluations beyond the mere predilections. In doing so, it seeks something akin to a World War II recognition silhouette; that is, it traces an outline for quick identification purposes, but does not seek to serve as a comprehensive description by any means.

This primer presents in four short parts: First, it affirmatively sets out the six positions or principles that appear more or less universally at the essence of Right-wing thought. Second, it sets out in broad brushstrokes how history is interpreted by most on the Right, *i.e.*, the story of the West down to today. Third, this work sets out six distinguishing views held by the Left. Finally, it offers the critique that the Right holds with respect to these latter viewpoints.

I. PRINCIPLES ON THE RIGHT

At the risk of reductionism, this work attempts a succinct characterization of the broad positions of the Right in the Western World.[3] It is beyond the scope of this work to address the abstractions or arguments that underlay them, but the following are a half dozen generally accepted core positions held across the political Right of today:

1. The Right rejects equality.
2. The Right affirms objective value.
3. The Right affirms the primacy of loyalty.
4. The Right is nationalist.
5. The Right asserts that conquest and domination are part of Progress.
6. The Right asserts that Western Civilization is currently, although not irrevocably, in decline.

---

3 Some on the list might have application in the world at large, to the Islamic world, to Africa and the Far East. However, others are self-evidently particular to the West.

1. *The Right rejects equality as a first principle of society; it affirms that hierarchy is natural.*

The Right assumes inequality, and even endorses it. Within real, organic, human and humane society, ranks and roles spring up naturally over time. The more complex the human association, the more complex its unwritten codes and organic hierarchy. Thus, there is no implicit duty for every man to accord equality to every other man. Indeed, quite the contrary. It would be unjust to do so.

It is not that some men are born to rule, or to thrive, or even that some men have more virtues than others do. Fundamentally, it is that no man is equivalent to any other man. Certainly no one is naturally entitled to social equality, nor, especially, to moral autonomy.

Moreover, treating the stranger as one's own kinsman is not only not required—it would be wrong to do so. Man is born within a particular family, people, and culture. To these he must defer, and from which he may by internal right demand deference in return.

10

Of course, the default presumption of equality is so pervasive today as to be ubiquitous, a piety that is even poisoning the well of Christianity from the point of view of the Right. Nonetheless, the Right and Conservatism reject equality as a first principle of human society.

2. The Right affirms the existence of objective value.

Necessarily, this rejection of equality stems from, and originates with, a commensurate affirmation of objective values as such. Man is not the measure of all things, and men are not ends unto themselves. And even while it bears the imprint of unity, the Good exhibits a mysterious diversity. This diversity of objective good explains differentiation and hierarchy.

The Right asserts that the world has meaning, and that this meaning can be known. That is, between the mind of Man and the meaning of his surrounding reality, there is no insurmountable wall. Furthermore, meta-historically, Man's March of History should be oriented around pursuing the Good, the Beautiful, and the True, even if the goal is never fully realized, and even if periods of degeneration routinely arise.

3. The political Right believes loyalty to people and place is paramount, and it believes that governance must be subordinate to this principle in order to be legitimate.

While anti-egalitarianism is obviously a negative principle for the Right, loyalty is a positive one. Loyalty is an affirmative objective value. It is a Good. Crucially, while loyalty may be (or may not be) the result of a *quid pro quo*, it should not be mistaken for such an exchange. It is not a contractual relationship. Rather, it is a spirit of treating another in some sense as oneself. Extending one's identity over the other.

Loyalty begets trust. Trust begets civilization.

Loyalty for the Right is necessarily the first of socio-political principles. Solidarity. Relations. Before there is a decision-making mechanism or rights in any community, there must be an understanding of what, and of whom, the community consists. Under traditional conservative values, loyalty is based upon people and place, blood and soil.

True, felt kinships can exist to the extent that a person may experience a real, living, commonality between himself and his neighbor through not only blood, but also through language, culture, shared rites . . . even simply through expressions of mutual justice and charity. Nonetheless, political propositions are not the font of loyalty. They are not natal. Propositions may be conscious or unconscious, certain propositions socially accepted or socially decried, but in no way do they make a community by themselves, and certainly not a nation. For one thing, their intergenerational impermanence prevents it. Their enforcement as the basis of community makes only the ideological state, not a nation. Leaving aside whether or not there is legitimacy in the concept of the ideological state, the concept of the proposition nation is a fallacy. ***Such is not a nation.*** *Natio* refers to birth and implies blood.

Furthermore, regardless of whether the

state follows the nation, or the nation follows the state, the community is the raison d'être of government. The mode of governance is always secondary, even when it is the prime mover of community. Real humans loyal to one another, the organic community, its place and form, are paramount.

As a correlative with this principle, from the point of the view of the Right authority in a legitimate state arises not primarily as the result of self-serving choice. Legitimate governance, true governance, is an institutional expression of a living, differentiated, populace. It is not merely an agency for individual rights, much less a vehicle to aggressively expand liberal democracy.

Normatively, in a civil state, the legitimacy of governmental authority exists through prescription. However, initial authority exists by virtue of leadership. The Right thus necessarily recognizes the reality of the concept of the Law-Giver, whether in the form of an individual or otherwise.[4]

4. The Right champions nationalism and Western civilization, and it rejects globalism.

Mankind is not a unity. Men do not have an equal moral claim upon one other.

Rather, there are nested and overlapping spheres of obligation, from family to tribe, to profession, class, nation, creed, religion, and civilization. The man of the Right does not speak from the perspective of Humanity (à la Spinoza) when coming to judgments. He speaks from his own perspective, which is a real person perspective, an organic, human perspective.

Thus, under today's circumstances, the Right is necessarily nationalistic, or patriotic, particularly when compared to global

---

4 For instance, the only reason that Americans today live in a republic, and are not, for instance, citizens of a state in the British Commonwealth of Nations is due to a choice made by the ancestors of (some) American citizens long ago. Not due to a conscious choice made by Americans of today. This is prescription. It stems from the actions of the American "Founding Fathers," *i.e.*, the law-givers of 1776.

internationalism. As patriotism (from the word, *patria*) necessarily includes a nativist or ethnic component; thus, Conservatism in the Western world is rightly seen as the champion of European, *i.e.*, white, civilization. Furthermore, according to many on the Right this partisanship of European civilization has an objective as well as a subjective basis.

COMMENT

One important caveat worth noting is that those on the Right are not in unanimity in their bases for endorsing some form of nationalism or ethnocentrism today. Indeed, modern nationalism is not in fact originally a Right-wing phenomenon, but rather originated on the Left in its struggle against organic hierarchy. However, at this juncture nationalism's home is on the Right.

In endorsing nationalism (or, more-precisely, eschewing globalism), some on the Right warn of the dangers of a potential "clash of civilizations." Some others still, focus on a posited reality regarding differences in ethnicity, and the assumed implications thereof. Other Rightists openly balk at these positions however, emphasizing instead simply the particular over the abstract.

These last hold that, inasmuch as they are of a particular descent and ethnic lineage, it is only natural for them to identify as such, even as a supranational sentiment. Some indeed ultimately ground their roots of loyalty and feelings of solidarity simply on the personal as such. Those European Conservatives who continue to champion Christendom, feudalism, or monarchy, are typically of this latter mindset. What all on the Right are clearly united against is the proposition that Mankind is one race, of fungible peoples, of indistinguishably equal rights-bearing, autonomous individuals.

5. The Right believes in a march of history, and that this march of history has periodically included conquest and domination.

The word "Progress" can take on meanings other than those which it has been assigned by the Left. And certainly Progress implies more than just change. It implies beneficial change. In the meta-historical sense, the Right believes that Progress in the human condition has in fact occurred.[5]

Man in his rudimentary forms of the distant past, gave way by 2000 B.C. to vast, organic, civilized societies. Indeed, the raw expansion of the world's population of *homo sapiens*, increased knowledge over the millennia, technical and cultural improvements, and astounding advances in living conditions have continued down to this day. Such Progress has occurred through accumulation, *e.g.*, through the brilliance of a Copernicus added to his predecessors, through Da Vinci's techniques with the *Mona Lisa* built upon those of his cave drawing ancestors, through solar energy technology built upon the technology of coal-fired steam engines . . . from two people to seven

---

5 While some (Right Hegelians) attribute this progress as part of a *Weltgeist*, *see*, *e.g.*, Georg Wilhelm Friedrich Hegel, *The Phenomenology of the Spirit*, others, notably practicing Christians, are far more ambivalent, given that the Apocalypse is their expected eventual end of history (and being otherwise hostile to the pantheistic spirit of a *Weltgeist*).

billion. Negative aspects of the human condition that were commonplace centuries ago, *e.g.*, chattel slavery and rampant infant mortality, are displaced over time. Such scientific, artistic, technological, and humanistic examples of flourishing reflect accumulative developments in human knowledge and ability. In this sense at the very least, there can be no rational impetus to return to the past.

Accretion is a complex historical process however. Accretion, Progress, ultimately occurs through the triumph of the greater over the lesser, and this extends to human civilization. Hunter-gatherers are displaced by herders, and then by farmers, and then by city-states. Rome destroyed Carthage, and the former came to rule the West. In turn, other European tribes overran, and yet refreshed, the Roman vision. Thereafter, Europe came to dominate and lead the world. This was Progress, both for the West and for rest of the world.

That is, in the politico-social realm, Man's flourishing has been propelled by a March of History—a march that has necessarily included conquest and domination, *i.e.*, a rejection of equal consideration. Progress occurs via this March of History. This is true, whether of the Cro-Magnon over the Neanderthal, the unification of the Upper and Lower Nile by the Pharaoh Narmer, or the Spanish over the Aztecs. Could it have been otherwise? As to individual examples, perhaps. And certainly the Right may be willing to concede that violent conflict today, amongst nation-states, may be so irrational as to be obsolete.[6] Yet in any event, in the larger sweep of history no Progress occurs without the triumph of something over something else, of someone over someone else.

6. Today the West is experiencing degeneration.

All this Progress notwithstanding, like a building whose foundation has been invisibly

---

6 *See* Normal Angell, *The Great Illusion*, arguing that in an age when a community's flourishing comes less from acquiring resources than from export, it makes little sense to immiserate one's trading partners and potential investors/investment opportunities.

eaten by termites, Western Civilization today is experiencing moral and spiritual decline. According to some on the Right this **degeneration** began centuries ago with the adoption of the language of Liberalism and of other languages of the Left, but all now agree that it has accelerated in the last several decades to threaten the survival of the structure itself. Whether this crisis is part of an eschatological moment, or simply cyclical, no morally well-grounded man of the Right sees today's Western World progressing in uninterrupted general improvement. Technologically yes. Materially perhaps.

But politically . . . legally . . . morally . . . spiritually . . . No. Quite the contrary.

Objective standards of beauty decline, while rage and chaos ensue. In modern perception, "racism" (however this term is defined) has replaced sexual license as the greatest of social evils. Unsurprisingly, the native birthrate declines. Today, physical displacement, stemming from the adoption of the civic religion of the Enlightenment and the subsequent failure of nerve, threatens Western Civilization. Suez is lost. France and Frenchmen are betrayed in Algeria by that ironic collaborator Charles de Gaulle. Harold Macmillan's "Winds of Change" bring a storm of immigrants, temporarily enriching a corrupt and deracinated bourgeoisie lifestyle through cheap labor. Cities in the American South are evacuated by Southerners seeking to protect their progeny, and the U.S. Immigration Act of 1924 is replaced by that of 1965. Old South Africa—a European nation founded on the African Continent, which was at one time unmatched there economically and militarily— is betrayed from within and without, and overrun in 1990. Today, European capitals have become to some extent . . . no longer European. *Europa* has begun to contract. With respect to all these, says the Right, the West is degenerate.

In the Rightist mindset, it is self-evident that a self-negating and oikophobic revolution has at least temporarily occurred in the West, obtaining dominance in the political world.

Its contamination and complete control over Western media and academia is legend.[7] Those advancing its spread are sad collaborators, or at best willing dupes. An Eleanor Roosevelt or a Warren Court in the United States, a Sartre (and a de Beauvoir) in France, and more recently, an Angela Merkel in Germany; these are only unfortunate characters, monuments to the weakness and degeneration of a civilization. Nonetheless, the Right affirms that the decline is reversible, if the West can only regain its nerve.

---

7 For instance, it is increasingly a fact that when Western news outlets report on political violence, their attitudes fluctuate depending upon the source of the conflict. The Left may do evil, but the Right *is* evil. The Left must be understood. The Right however is simply pathological. The radical Left is . . . only radical. The extreme Right is however, an existential threat. But the question must be asked, an existential threat to whom?

II. HISTORY AND ITS MEANING, AS SEEN FROM THE RIGHT

A consensus in current Anthropology teaches that the *homo* genus originated in Africa in the distant past and eventually spread throughout the world, first to the Eastern Hemisphere, then to the Western. Some anthropologists further claim that eventually one species of the genus—*homo sapiens*, Man—much later also left Africa, moving northward up that continent's eastern coastline, establishing societies both nomadic and settled, along the shores it traveled. And that this Man continued along the Indian Ocean littoral and beyond.[8]

---

8 These theories seem to imply that, if *homo sapiens* at times mated with different local populations of the *homo* genus in different parts of the world, then the modern human species would perforce be somewhat genetically distinctive from place to place. This point notwithstanding however, *homo sapiens* has been defined from time immemorial as the "rational animal," and not by DNA.

Whether these claims are true or not, or whether all men, in all their diversity, came down more recently from Mt. Ararat in the Caucasus Mountains as the progeny of Noah; it is nonetheless clear that Europeans, whatever they looked like, expanded throughout their continent millennia ago. These proto-Europeans migrated into, and laid claim to, lands still partially frozen over by an Ice Age. Their original populations seem to have extended between the regions of the Polar North down to the shores of the Caspian Sea. Even as Semitic peoples moved out into the Middle East and North Africa, even as Asians moved across the vastness of Eurasia, eventually to reach the Pacific Ocean and the Americas, even as Africans remained and spread throughout that continent; *Europa* was born.

Well before 1000 B.C., the Celts began expanding throughout Europe to the Pillars of Hercules. Likewise, the Nordic/Germanic peoples began their slow dispersal out of Scandinavia. The proto-Slavic peoples began habitation of the eastern steppes. And certainly by 1000 B.C., the most civilized Europeans (the Greeks) had settled into city-states, founding these upon the Achaean peninsula. These city-states formed the basis of what would eventually become Western Civilization.

Primordial Man throughout the world, to include European Man, held fealty to his gods and idols, as instrumentalities in his life. Instruments for a good harvest or a good hunt. Instruments for fecundity and childbirth. Instruments for honor and glory. However, the Ancient Greeks eventually began to ask questions such as: "Why?" "What for?" These questions were not unique to the Greeks, but their answers arguably were.

Greek civilization reasoned its way from pantheism to various propositions of objective value. With Platonism, the Greek further reasoned to the conclusion that the world's origin was unitary, necessarily contained all perfections, and lay apart from Creation. Some others still, concluded that the relation of reality to its origin, and the explanation of change within reality, is something that could be characterized as purposive causation. Telos.

Synthesizing the religion of the ancient Hebrews, the Greco-Roman world would eventually endorse the idea that the origin of all that exists was not only good, but also a personality. Intelligent and intelligible. Thereby engendering objective value. Is and ought.

The West would endorse the idea that the flaws evident in human nature were due to Man's deviation from the plan of his Creator. Ultimately, through the Creator's own example, sacrifice was the expression of, and only route to, a return to plan, to a resurrection. Embracing sacrifice of the Self (something of objective value, and of ultimate subjective value) for the Good—transforming the hero into the saint—arose as the common *religio* of European civilization, and spread throughout the whole world.

This obviously refers to Christianity.

It must be noted here that some on today's Right fault the Western embrace of Christianity. With Nietzsche, they see Christianity as a servile, self-negating religion. Further, tracing their roots back to Nietzsche, and perhaps through Jung and Voegelin, they criticize its premise of objectivity.

Others maintain however, that objectivity is a *sine qua non* for classification on the Right. In any event, it is difficult to imagine Western or modern European identity historically divorced from Christianity. Whether the secular Right and liberal Christians have Christianity correct, or whether traditional Christianity and the radical Left are more accurate on the subject; these are questions of faith and theology that are not pertinent here. The fact remains that the vast majority of Conservatives in the West self-identify at least somewhat as Christian, and these Christian Conservatives take pains to distinguish between self-sacrifice on one hand, and self-negation on the other. Whether the intra-Right dispute is real or only semantic is beyond the scope of this primer.[9]

For most of human civilization, indeed in the five or six thousand years of recorded

---

9 Certainly all on the Right agree that, with Modernity something like Nietzsche's Great Nausea has set in.

history, the peoples and cradles of civilization remained relatively unconnected with one another. Then beginning around 1500 A.D., Europe effectively exploded across the planet, spreading throughout it, and interconnecting it. Dominating it. Domination of the planet by Western Civilization is part of the Progress of Man.[10]

Domination and conquest are the assertion of will, of being, over a space. Indeed, ownership of, and sovereignty over, land, natural resources, even over one's own self, is asserting by definition the right to exclude the will of another. Of course, ownership is a function in the first instance of the need to own. Own something, food, resources, labor, whatever. But overarching this need is the will, and the ability, to dominate. To lay a claim, and say, "this is mine." The Right endorses this will. It avers that personal property, properly

---

10 Although Herder's admonitions against conquest, and the snuffing out of other cultures that may yet flourish, are well-taken by some Rightists.

personal property

conditioned, is a natural Good.[11] It avers that political sovereignty is a natural Good. These dominations, these Goods, are part of the March of History.

Like his Roman forebears, after 1500 A.D. modern European man oversaw empire. According to the Right, it is beyond question that he eventually oversaw a historically unique, global fecundity. European conquest oversaw the closure (at least theoretically) of markets of enslavement like those of Timbuktu where forfeited lives were traded. It eventually oversaw child-birth made relatively safe for the child-bearer throughout the world. It oversaw a green revolution. It has overseen Western arts, sciences, and thought take a place of dominance in the world. These are Goods.[12]

The Right asks for instance, how many non-Europeans are alive today who would not be,

---

11 In contrast, the Left has historically oscillated between considering property sacrosanct, to abolishing it altogether.

12 To call these "Goods" (which of course could be a debatable conclusion), is to acknowledge that there is such a thing as Man, even if the Right does not concede his fungibility.

save that some European in the past conquered their ancestors?[13] Who may complain of Westerners, except by standing upon their shoulders? This was the March of History. The Right will not condemn it, nor apologize for it.

Unlike the universalist Left, the Right explicitly, necessarily, embraces diversity. However, this does not translate to embracing moral relativism. As with all human relations, just as refusing to accord equality where it is due would be an injustice, so too would be to treat as equal that which is not. And the Right in the West believes in the West, holding that the West moves generally in history toward the Good, Beautiful, and True.

Modernity has seen the West stumble. For instance, most recently during the Age of Enlightenment, an ironic darkening of thought

----

13 As opposed, for instance, to the alternative, to acting as humans have in other times and places. Today who speaks for the innumerable human tribes wiped out in the distant past, *e.g.*, the Midianites of the Bible, or for that matter, the Neanderthal or *homo floresiensis*? These human lineages no longer exist, and thus they cannot be heard to complain today of their ill-treatment in the past.

demanded reexamination and justification of prior Western judgments, evaluations, and hierarchies. Of course, questioning or requiring justification is not a bad thing, in and of itself. But upon what grounds to judge without belief in Truth itself? That is, an incessant demand for justification arose as Europeans began to doubt the attainability of metaphysical truths, *i.e.*, Truth.[14]

Inevitably, the insatiable demand for justification resulted in denying human inequality *tout court*. In the pre-Enlightenment era, the nature of Goods and their relative "goodness," were topics that could be subject to question. Further, whether the prevailing hierarchical structure tailored itself to the promotion of the Good was also open to theoretical debate, potentially upsetting any particular circumstance of inequality. However, Post-Enlightenment, with no Truth in Goods or Beauty to serve as a gauge, there exists no bases to answer with a theoretical justification

---

14 *See* Immanuel Kant, *Critique of Pure Reason*.

for human inequality of any kind. Without the capacity to ground hierarchy or a structure of values on objective Truth, equality replaces inequality as the default.

This result was made the more inevitable by the fact that, while what constitutes the Good may always be up for debate post-Enlightenment, the same has not proven necessarily true as to what constitutes Evil. We do not know the Good, but we do seem to know universally what we don't like: Pain and deprivation. We are for nothing. But we are against pain and deprivation, and these are universally equal concerns.[15] Goods, on the other hand, are for the post-Enlightened man, simply subjective.

In contrast, for the Right the existence of positive divine archetypes requires no justification, so it will not foreswear pursuing the Good. On the island of the blind, the one-eyed man is king by right. The Right refuses to justify nature . . . being . . . beauty . . . love

---

15 *See, e.g.*, Richard Rorty, *Achieving our Country*.

. . . identity . . . Thus, by extension the Right rejects equality, equal consideration, as an *à priori* premise of Man.

Critics of the Right have objected, not surprisingly, that this belief in objective, knowable, truth is a prescription, not only for inequality, but also for endless conflict, as well as oppression.[16] Anyone who claims to have the Truth would be morally self-empowered in seeking to impose it on others.

The Right asks in turn however, how is this more sanguinary than modern conflicts where objective Truths and Goods are absent as goals? How are wars fought to liberate a people from oppression (at least ostensibly), or fought pursuant to some kind of Hegelian dialectic, less bloody? Or how is the Right's position more sanguinary than the age-old conflicts driven simply by natural egocentrism—the only principle remaining when metaphysical

---

16 The European wars of religion during the 16th and 17th centuries are perhaps paradigmatic examples.

Truth is banished?[17]

Moreover, if nothingness and agnosticism are the only alternatives, then conflict and war are indeed preferable for the Right. That is, it not only disputes the validity of the assertions made by John Lennon in his bleak ballad *Imagine*; for the Right, Lennon is in fact describing the *Inferno*, rather than a *Paradiso*. Seen from this perspective, the conflict between the Right and Left today takes on the characteristics of a religious conflict.

How does the Right explain the current degeneration of the West? After European Man assumed a leadership of the world and established the very grounds upon which to complain, the Right is forced to ask itself, why the decline? If white civilization is as impressive as its proponents boast, why is it so pathetic and defenseless now? After marching from Parthenon to rocket ship, from Mozart to the

---

17 In a secular-nihilist world, how can a duty arise to respect some sanctity in the human person? Apart from offering discredited justifications such as atemporal game theory or feeble tautologies? Logically one cannot deny an objective Natural Law and at the same time rely upon its application.

radio . . . how did this happen? After conquering and colonizing, or temporarily overawing other venerable civilizations, even such as India and China . . . how did this happen? And when did the decline really start?

The Right is not of one mind on the answers to any of these questions. As to the former questions (How? Why?), some point to cycles in history. Others blame Marxism, the French Revolution, the two world wars, the Enlightenment of course, or even the Reformation and Renaissance. As alluded to previously, a few even blame Christianity itself.

As to the latter question (When?), many on the Right identify the spiritual decline as beginning in the Late Middle Ages, as evidenced by the abandonment, first of the Holy Land, and then of Byzantium. They claim that the true faith and transcendent identity of Europe were shaken to their roots at this time. A rising neurosis progressively separated the world into its modular components, faith and reason, church and state, things and intellect, Man and Nature. Whether the darkness arose from the failure of Romano-European unity, internal corruptions, from failures against Islam, or, perhaps simply out of the devastation wrought by the Great Plague; it heralded the leveling counter-cult of today.

Self-evidently, the various Rightists are in consensus with each other in their rejection of moral relativism, and the anti-civilization aspects of Liberalism and of the Left generally. It is this perceived relativism and degeneration against which all on the Right intransigently set their faces.

The Right sees today as a task, another step in an ongoing crusade for the Good, the Beautiful, and the True. This crusade is a journey rather than an endpoint. And it has its opponents. While Western Civilization produced modern democracy (as well as capitalism), for the Right today's self-referential liberal state has elevated itself into a thing of worship, and has become at times demonic. According to the dogmatically pluralist and secular political leadership of the West, liberal democracy is simply autotelic, not open for debate. The

Popular Front has ascended, and hypocritically taken up the ladder behind it. Asking questions and dissenting from the liberal state, looking for something more, are consigned now to the status of, ironically-enough, the Other, "the Enemy."[18]

Yet, today, liberal democracy is itself in crisis. What if its practice leads to the dissolution of the people, of the nation . . . of the community's welfare, traditions, religious spirit, and order? What if its practice leads to the dissolution of the person? And if liberal democracy threatens these calamities, what is its value? Can it be reformed? These questions do not produce easy answers, but it seems that only the Right acknowledges the legitimacy of the questions. In sum, for the Right, 2016 was a year of hope.

---

18 *See* Carl Schmitt, *The Concept of the Political.*

III. PRINCIPLES ON THE LEFT

In opposing the Left, the Right does not have trouble in recognizing the positions of its opponent. Those positions, whether in the West or in the rest of the world, are very recognizable, often thoughtfully expressed, and their supporters are well disposed to explain and defend them. However, the Right has difficulty in fully engaging with these positions, due in large part to a failure to recognize that they are further grounded in more deeply held abstractions.

There exists a unifying underlying worldview for the Left, perceived as self-evident, and providing the basis for the Left's cleavage with the Right. While the primary purpose of this work is to explore the principles of the Right, nonetheless it is expedient to set forth the fundamental principles of the Left, in order to examine how the Right reacts to these positions and to their underlying worldview. Again, at the risk of reductionism, the following appear to be the six generally accepted core principles held across the political Left of today:

1. The Left demands justification for political choice.

2. The Left asserts that an empirical basis is required for justification.

3. The Left is egalitarian.

4. The Left is universalist.

5. For the Left, Progress means the lifting of imposition.

6. In pursuing Progress, the modern West has achieved ever-higher states of perfection.

1. & 2. The Left requires justification in accordance with empirical facts, of all political perspectives.

The Left, not just in politics but more generally as well, can be boiled down to one indispensable attribute in both philosophy and temperament: Justification. The Left is fundamentally constituted in the drive to find justification, and to arrive at justifications from a standpoint of epistemological/metaphysical humility. The ramifications of the Left project—to include coming to judgments as to its permutations—can only be interpreted in the light of this observation.[19]

This drive for justification is intertwined with, or perhaps preceded by, another bedrock Left principle: Only the empirical qualifies as knowledge.

A person can measure the length of an object and communicate her findings with another, and that other person can perfectly share in this knowledge through empirical verification. The same cannot be said of non-empirical, speculative, and purpose-premised knowledge.

Rationally, knowledge pertains only to those judgments that accord with empirical facts, *i.e.*, scientific materialism. In contrast,

---

19 As such, when two Left positions conflict, one is inevitably seen as more authentically Left than the other, *e.g.*, Feminism versus Transgenderism. One is more justifiable than the other in the eyes of the Left. In contrast, there is not necessarily a more Rightist position when two groups on the Right collide, *e.g.*, French nationalism versus German nationalism.

affirming anything to be Good, Beautiful, or True—the pursuit of which is perhaps the principle at the heart of the Right—involves radically subjective judgments.

The Left does not go so far as to assert that knowledge is limited to physical phenomena however. Principles of logic such as cause and effect, conservation of mass-energy, even good versus evil, love versus hate, are all propositions acceptable to the Left practically speaking. The point is that physically measurable phenomena delimit what may count as evidence. Only universal, measurable, criteria may be used as a gauge. While Man may not be the only animal that questions—other animals, to be sure, engage in decision-making, and may be capable of complex mental processes—Man is the only animal that evinces not only the ability to question his surroundings, but also the propensity to project meaning onto those surroundings. For the Left, this projection is fraught with danger, and with error. Practically speaking, regarding questions of ethical or political import, such matters are legitimately addressable only under the aegis of scientific materialism.

The Left does not defy the common sense of Mankind gratuitously. It does not normally evince a dispassionate, subjective attitude when making pedestrian observations or comparisons, *e.g.*, the joys of parenthood versus the pain of enduring a stillbirth, the beauty of the Grand Canyon versus the view of a dilapidated strip mall. Nonetheless, the materialist attitude becomes more glaring the more dissenters are willing to come forward. A glass of Grand Vin de Chateau Latour may be called "superior" to a can of Miller Lite, in caloric terms (approximately 125 to 95), or in terms of alcoholic content (approximately 14% to 4.2%). However, characterizing the former as superior, in a qualitative way, would be meaningless to the Left, as some people may just prefer Miller Lite.[20] Bordeaux wine, claret, is not "better." Thus, by extrapolation,

---

20 *See, e.g.*, Dworkin, Ronald. "What Is Equality? Part 1: Equality of Welfare." *Philosophy and Public Affairs* 10, no. 3 (1981): 185-246.

characterizing homosexuality or bare sexual promiscuousness as perverse or immoral would constitute not only an error according to the Left, but also a characterization without foundation, *i.e.*, essentially ignorant gibberish, unworthy of consideration.

Humanity is flung into this world as finite beings in a finite universe with finite resources, and, as such, people must reason together. If we must reason together, then Reason must be our guide. Reason pertains to analyzing the efficacy of a process to reach a result. It cannot determine purpose in anything in itself. There is no legitimate, speculative "Reason" to determine such ends,[21] so the process is limited to the empirical. Succinctly put, all ***values*** are relative. None is objective.

Who is to say what is good? Or true? And beauty is famously said to be in the eyes of the beholder. Any affirmation of the Good,

---

21 According to Etienne Gilson, Auguste Comte believed that "Scientists never ask themselves ***why*** things happen, but ***how*** they happen." Etienne Gilson, *God and Philosophy* (emphasis in the original).

the Beautiful, or the True inevitably involves a component that is teleological at best, or hedonic at worst, one which begs the question not only of the accuracy of the judgment, but more importantly, of the existence of meaning and purpose altogether.

The Right, of whatever shade, respects both empirical and non-empirical knowledge, arriving at evaluations, *i.e.*, "Values," that the Right calls objective. The Left demurs as to the latter type of knowledge, to judgments premised upon a non-empirical, teleological premise. The Left asserts then, that it is only reasonable to resolve this conflict by positing consensus in accepting scientific materialism and the empirical, while agreeing to disagree on the teleological, speculative, and non-empirical.

The Right cannot avoid the fact that asserting purpose to existence, even upon some evidence, requires a leap of faith, and the Left's epistemological/metaphysical humility reflects a sincere skepticism for which the reasonable person has to have some sympathy. Further, the Left's reaction and hostility to the Right's tenets (on the theoretical level) reflect equally reasonable concerns at least inasmuch as the Right's dogged persistence in belief in objective Values is an imposition upon, as well as an indictment (felt to be unjust) of, the Left's very sober lack of credulity.

COMMENT

It should be pointed out here that the Left's epistemological skepticism does not have a historical pedigree as ancient as that of its opponent. While Socrates may have been the questioner par excellence of the belief in objective knowledge, he did not arrive at the same conclusions as does the modern Left. And while there have been realist skeptics from Democritus to Proclus in the West, theirs was a metaphysical disputation rather than an epistemological one. The Left today is in large part, ironically, a reactionary offspring of the Western intellectual tradition, at least from the Enlightenment onward.

Indeed, in concrete terms, the year 1919 is

as good a date as any, to choose for the point at which the Left – Right confrontation as it exists today was first framed, when principles from the abortive 1848 European revolution were made norms, and given worldwide application. Even if an earlier date is chosen, it becomes difficult to make an argument for a Left intellectual position predating the Cartesian revolution.

3. The Left postulates equality.

According to the Left, all Values are subjective, as qualitative "knowledge" is in reality mere preference masquerading as objectivity. And there are no "better" or "worse" preferences. Human equality is the necessary result of this conclusion, of Man's profound ignorance regarding the existence of meaning in the universe. As such, the free choices of equal participants must be the default rule of social interaction.[22]

No overarching human archetype or mode of life is superior, and no objective measure

---

22 *See* Bruce Ackerman, *Social Justice in the Liberal State.*

above that of the individual *homo sapiens* is recognizable. Any other conclusion is, again, mere preference. Qualitative differences, *e.g.*, rank, are social accretions, of illegitimate birth. Relational predilections, *e.g.*, race . . . nation . . . tribe . . . family, are irrational, ultimately unjustifiable, prejudices.

As to qualitative distinctions, while a person's abilities may be a benefit to that person, it is unjustifiable for those abilities to impose themselves as social privilege.[23] So that, even though human nature may produce admiration for certain archetypes, as well as produce certain affinities for progeny, these are only gut reactions, and ultimately irrational. There is no "Good" in human qualifications. Neither is there fundamentally a "Good" in the family, or in extended kinships, *e.g.*, the tribe.[24]

---

23 *See* Robert Nozick, *Anarchy, State, and Utopia.*

24 For instance, it is reputed that Samuel Adams disavowed inheritance as a just manner to obtain wealth. Rather, all men should be of sorts, "self-made." Apparently, in like mind, Warren Buffet has reportedly given away much of his liquid wealth, rather than bequeathing it to his family.

Again, equal human dignity and consideration is the only rational rule for the one human family.

How does Man go from the radical epistemological principle of empiricism, to assert that at the heart of human society and of the polity is mandated equality? As opposed to benevolent equality, why are not anarchy and nihilism the inescapable conclusions in the search for social justice from the agnostic position—justice understood as the way things "ought" to be?[25]

In *A Theory of Justice*—taking an obvious cue from Immanuel Kant—Liberal philosopher John Rawls offers one escape. He proposes that justice as "fairness" requires assuming the position that the subject person make political evaluations and decisions from behind a

_____

25 In *A Brief History of Humankind*, taking as given a materialistic and evolutionary view of history, author Yuval Noah Harari arguably points up the fact that morality from the materialist perspective can be seen, at best, as an observation, and, in likely truth, simply an invention.

theoretical "Veil of Ignorance."[26] Behind this veil, the person is kept ignorant of her sex, her religion, her status, her virtues and vices, or any of the other attributes otherwise making up her personhood. Only from behind a veil of knowledge should she make the social, political, and economic decisions affecting herself and others. Thereby equality replaces nihilism.

COMMENT

As a pertinent aside, one matter the Right has consistently failed to grasp in the past is that freedom and equality are not fundamentally polar opposites in the abstract. Freedom and equality are in fact simply two sides of the same coin, as human equality at root simply means for all humans to be equally free. Indeed, the Left starts from a position where freedom, choice, is sacrosanct. Autonomy is untouchable. But one must ask oneself: What are the conditions by which this equal freedom could be made possible?

Although required in the abstract, for the

26 *See* John Rawls, *A Theory of Justice.*

Left human equality does not comport with practical human license. This conclusion may seem understandable enough in terms of commission. One cannot exercise one's freedom by affirmatively imposing oneself over another, without also doing injury to the principle of freedom at the same time. No freedom worthy of the name is possible in a violent anarchy. That is, respecting the "freedom" to use force is not really respecting freedom at all. "[N]o man has a natural authority over his fellow, and force creates no right."[27] To that extent at least, the freedoms of at least some are curtailed, in order to facilitate the equal freedoms of all.

Yet, this idea of curtailing practical freedom necessarily holds in terms of omission, as well as commission, under the Rawlsian regime. This is so because individual persons require cooperation from each other, require society for survival, and resources are finite. "First in time" is no justification. One who unjustifiably omits aid to another is impermissibly peeking

---

27 Jean Jacques Rousseau, *The Social Contract*, Book 1, ¶ IV.

around the Veil of Ignorance. Thus, Humanity is commanded to be sociable with his fellows.

After all, behind the veil, no one would know if he just might need some help or resources from his fellows. The logical result of this point is that J. S. Mills' famous aphorism, "your liberty to swing your fist ends just where my nose begins," turns into the equally famous diktat commonly accredited to Karl Marx, "from each according to his ability, to each according to his needs."

Boiled down, freedom for the Left means fundamentally the freedom to be self-defining, *i.e.*, to define one's desires and thus purposes. Free from all external dictates. Self-actualization. Man is imbued with the "right to define one's own concept of existence, of the universe, and of the mystery of human life."[28] Not coincidentally this is the one freedom that the Right intrinsically denies.

The Veil of Ignorance has many practical

---

28 This quote is from the Majority Opinion in the U.S. Supreme Court abortion case, *Planned Parenthood of Southeastern Pennsylvania v. Casey*, 505 U.S. 833, 851 (1992).

ramifications. For instance, national borders arguably become unjustifiable. From behind the veil, the Left asks how can one deny entry or citizenship to those who have a need for resources located within the polity? Economic inequality, social inequality, respect for gender roles, these all become irrational, unjustifiable choices for the person behind the veil.

Additionally, how can it be just for the previous generation to impose on its offspring (even simply by the monopoly on inculcation, which parents currently have over their children) the previous generation's way of life and Values, including the previous generation's religion? If the offspring are by right equal in dignity to their forebears, the former have a right to determine their own ways of life and Values free from the constraints of their parents. The state has the duty to respect and potentially enforce this right. "If the parents in this case are allowed a religious exemption, the inevitable effect is to impose the parents' notions of religious duty upon their children . . . . [I]t would be an invasion of the child's rights to permit such an imposition without canvassing his views."[29]

According to the Left, it is part of the purpose of law to serve as a corrective to inequality (and it should certainly not reinforce it). To cite an example, the pro-choice position, aka Reproductive Justice, begins from the quite reasonable proposition that pregnancy is a physical burden upon the body, and thus an added one for women. That is, nature does not compel pregnancy upon men. Therefore, the law cannot be justified in compelling it upon women, who should be free to abort their pregnancies without limitation, out of respect for their equality.

4. *The Left postulates universalism.*

The Left is oriented around and committed to justification, scientific materialism, and by extension to equality. It is also committed to the universality of these principles.

---

29 This quote is from the Dissenting Opinion of Justice Douglas in the U.S. Supreme Court Amish case, *Wisconsin v. Yoder*, 406 U.S. 205, 242 (1972).

As noted, humans are ignorant of the content or even the existence of objective purpose, and thus all persons and Values must be viewed as equal. At the same time, men and women are finite beings in need of resources for survival, and crucially, they are in need of cooperation, again as noted above. By virtue of this need for cooperation, sociability, every human act **or omission** must be theoretically justifiable to every other individual human. In short, there exists a default rule of inclusion, and this rule is universal. Again, Humanity is commanded to be sociable.

Barriers to inclusion provide the one and only theoretical ground for complaint. The grounds of rational consent—and illegitimate dissent— are set. For instance, if homosexual society acts inclusively with respect to heterosexuals, this is all that the latter have a right to expect. Heterosexuals cannot complain that they wish to exclude homosexuals from their community, but are prevented from doing so. People have a right to complain if they are treated unequally. No one has a normative right to complain that he is being treated equally, or forced to treat others with like, equal consideration.

Moreover, because the rule is universal, those resisting this rule of inclusion are not justified in doing so. To the contrary, the demands of justification require that any such opposition to inclusion be suppressed. So, ironically perhaps, even while excluders are commanded to include, they themselves may be excluded. This is sometimes called the Tolerance Paradox. The Left affirms however, that this is not a paradox.

> I do not imply, for instance, that we should always suppress the utterance of intolerant philosophies; as long as we can counter them by rational argument and keep them in check by public opinion, suppression would certainly be unwise. But **we should claim the right to suppress them if necessary even by force**; for it may easily turn out that they are not prepared to meet us on the level of rational argument, but begin by denouncing all argument; they may forbid their followers to listen to rational argument, because it is deceptive, and teach them to answer arguments by the use of their

fists or pistols. ***We should therefore claim, in the name of tolerance, the right not to tolerate the intolerant.***[30]

For the Left, diversity with regard to opinions on inclusiveness, would be an oxymoron and self-defeating. Society permits itself to be challenged, but only according to the lights of tolerance. Logically, this limitation upon the freedom to dissent is justifiable of course, only if the tolerant society is in fact substantively superior to the "intolerant" one.

According to the Left, the tolerant society is in fact self-evidently superior. The individual person, having the dignity of his or her Humanity, is entitled to work out his or her own version of "the Good." Thus, the goal, and only goal, of society is material prosperity, and it is logical for only the tolerant to be treated unconditionally with tolerance, just as Karl Popper suggests. All others, depending upon

---

30 Karl Popper, *The Open Society and its Enemies*. In addition to Karl Popper, *see* Herbert Marcuse, *Repressive Tolerance*, and a myriad of others. Liberal freedom is logical only for liberal choices.

circumstances, may be treated intolerantly—
that is, it is a <u>universal rule that you must give
tolerance in order to receive tolerance.</u>

5. & 6. *In transcending itself, the West is achieving progress.*

With the Right, the <u>Left also famously believes
in Progress</u>, but it is a Progress in a form radically
differing from that of the Right. The Right sees
Progress as something accumulated, whether
materially so or otherwise. To use an example,
the Right may see progress in the institutions
of governance, when monarchy gives way to a
republic of the few, and from such a republic to
universal democracy, all by virtue of advances
in communications, education, and material
prosperity. These latter are progress in the
material realm. Additionally, the evolution
to democratic governance may potentially be
regarded as moral progress as well, to the extent
that the many gain the ability to legitimately
participate in the government of the whole.
That is, Rightist Progress translates to the ever-
increasing sum of qualitative knowledge and

ability.

In contrast, for the Left Progress is fundamentally viewed as the removal of impediments. It means the removal of natural impediments to be sure, *e.g.*, hunger and disease. More importantly however, it means removing the irrational corruptions and oppressions of the ages, purifying Humanity's existence from unjustifiable accretions. In some sense it means returning to a Monism from human (a pre-lapsarian?) pre-existence. It means getting back to the unencumbered human individual, back to the point where increasing openness and indeterminacy reign, and where no one is shackled by the accidents of birth. The innocent, nonalienated state. Under such a view, democracy would represent progress because the irrational prejudices producing the prior hierarchical order are swept away in favor of returning to a primordial Humanity. Equality is not a condition to be gained; rather it is a condition to be unveiled.

For the Left, Progress is a return to the human individual in all of his or her potential.

It is the scraping of the hull of Humanity of its accumulated injustices and reducing the influence of the non-empirical, the so-called knowledge of objective Values. It is an unwinding of the immodest perception of knowledge in myth-laden transcendent truths.

Therefore, Progress means the increasing willingness and ability of individual persons to live without inherited, discovered, or revealed purpose. People must make their own purposes, be their own authors, or at least find such things within themselves.[31] They must find their desires within themselves, without recourse to supposed objective reality and meaning outside themselves. Those who require received purpose from outside themselves are examples of the deformed "authoritarian personality."[32] Therefore, a truly progressive, liberated society would be a society of communal welfare, but

---

31 Viewed in this light, the motto of the State of New Hampshire, "Live Free or Die," becomes less a declaration and more of a threat.

32 The Frankfurt School popularized this notion. *See, e.g.,* Erich Fromm, *Escape from Freedom.*

otherwise, a free market regarding personal Values. Material collectivism, but moral anarchy.

For centuries, Humanity has benefited from Liberal Progress. Since at least the Renaissance and Reformation, history has been on the axiomatic path of Progress, of revolutionary return.[33] Democracy has emerged as the sole legitimate form of governance, to which even today's most hard-bitten dictator or theocrat must pay lip service. Constitutionalism, fundamental rights, secularism, and the parliamentary form have triumphed within democracy. In governance, process has replaced the Right's Quixotic pursuit of "ultimate ends" as the yardstick of measuring legitimacy. Pluralism and equality have displaced superstitious faith and Western identity as the glue of Western public virtue. All social roles, to include those of gender and age, have been, or are in the

---

33 The putative man on the Left, too, can be an imbiber in a belief in the *Weltgeist. See, e.g.*, Pierre Teilhard de Chardin, S.J., *The Phenomenon of Man*; Yuval Noah Harari, *A Brief History of Humankind*.

process of being, toppled. These advances are threatened by the resurgent, illiberal Right, and it is for this reason that the Left cannot afford to misunderstand its opponent.

IV. HOW THE LEFT FAILS, ACCORDING TO THE RIGHT

The Right affirms certain propositions as objective Values, and it does so in terms of the purported Good, the Beautiful, and the True. By extension it endorses inequality and the March of History. One of the practical objective values is loyalty, which also by extension encompasses the populist nationalism of today. The very existence of the Left stems to some degree from a reaction to, and a rejection of, these propositions. Unsurprisingly, the Right does not find the Left's bases for rejection compelling.

From the Left perspective, the principles of the Right and the permutations therefrom are mere exclusionary "preferences" passing themselves off as objective Values. These preferences are unjustifiable, and the Right in fact does not try to justify them in any fundamentally neutral, empirical way. The Left project revolves around doing away with such irrational preferences. From preference itself.

The Right objects to this, calling it special pleading. To attack "preferences" *per se*, is nonsense. Choices of any kind, on any basis, imply exclusion. They negate the equality of the excluded. For the Left, they must be justifiable on empirically neutral grounds, at least to the extent such choices pertain to people. The practical upshot of this requirement is that many populist outcries, such as, for example, "France for the French," constitute unjustifiable positions in the eyes of the Left.[34]

---

34 In the eyes of the Left a legitimate governor ultimately does not govern in the name of the nation. Rather, he administers the nation in the name of a human imperium. The governor's edicts must be justifiable to all, even though those edicts reach only to the borders of the province. "Give me your tired, your poor, your huddled masses yearning to breathe free" (quote from the base of the Statue of Liberty in New York City harbor—a gift from republican France, but a controversial one at the time of its dedication in 1886) is a rational plea only where the entirety of Mankind is the constituent.

The fatal flaw in the Left's critique from the Rightist perspective is that the former's project results in a preference as well, one equally unjustifiable from a neutrally empirical standpoint, and certainly not from a Right standpoint. That is, as opposed to the Right, *the Left fails according to its own lights*.

The Left claims to be ruled by the social principle of free choice, among equal and equally-situated participants, and that it is strictly neutral regarding the truly private, the personally human. But the Right points out that all this procedural fealty produces only an insoluble paradox because, under the Left's own logic, all choices made by people . . . affect people, *i.e.*, others.

The Leftist rejection of objective Value exalts choice, self-actualization, but this rejection ends implicitly, and sometimes explicitly, in condemning every concrete exercise of choice. It is not possible to choose to pursue a particular good,[35] and certainly not possible to live in a

---

35 To use a different kind of example, for a couple to choose to have a baby, or to have many babies, is a commitment, and

particularized community, without excluding some alternative. Such a choice would involve discrimination. This result is, theoretically speaking, unacceptable *per se* for the Left.

Thus, as a practical matter then, Liberalism *ad absurdum* refuses to say—or permit anyone else to say—what is valuable. So the Left goes from condemning the Right's illusions of objective Value, to condemning evaluation altogether. The only rational choice under the Left's logic would be to have choice but not to exercise it, because choice involves excluding a something other, a someone other.

In contrast, the Right only acknowledges what it also deems to be self-evident: Exclusion is the fundamental attribute of all choice,

---

it is in some sense an imposition both upon the couple and upon society. For one thing, it is a denial of adoption to an infant from an impoverished country. In contrast, choosing to have an abortion is not a choice in the same way. Instead, it is declining to making the same kind of commitment; it is choosing to leave one's options open, *status quo ante*. The couple have a right to, can always choose to, have a baby, but they forebear from doing so because that would involve losing their childless freedom. Such a mode of analysis is only possible of course, because considerations for the fetus are disregarded.

of all values "private" or "public" (and, not incidentally, of property and sovereignty as well). The Right affirms that it is the **products** of choice, properly qualified, not the mere potential for choice itself, that constitute natural Goods. To return to the point, if freedom translates into a Good, it must be conceded that there is no freedom, without the freedom to exclude.

The Right's rejection of liberal egalitarianism—to the extent it is grounded upon the Veil of Ignorance—is perhaps more straightforward. The decision to extend the veil over the set of every *homo sapiens*, equally, but over nothing else, is an explicit species of special pleading.

The Right asks: Why this exact set? Even setting aside the fact that every real person[36] born is unique, with his own ethnicity, sex, history, likes and dislikes, etc. . . . as part of his very ground of being as a human; perhaps more damning, there remains the question

---

36 However "person" is defined.

of how can the person behind the theoretical veil assume knowledge *à priori*, as to whether he is a *homo sapiens* as opposed to something else.[37] Behind the veil I am not supposed to know if I am a man or woman, an African or a Ukrainian, a celebrity or a pauper. Why am I supposed to know that I am a human being, and not a dolphin, a tree, a mountain, or even pure potentiality? How is this knowledge of the latter justifiable?

While logically the metaphysically blindfolded person would seemingly need to demonstrate justification for preferring *homo sapiens* over other animals, life over non-life, or being over non-being; nonetheless, the Left ignores this as a consideration. The individual human person is the Alpha and Omega of the Liberal, Rawlsian construction (for the time being at least[38]), apparently because

---

37 Or a person in the world, as opposed to a fetus in the womb.

38 Others have posited an ethic of duty based upon whether the object in question can feel pain, accusing Humanity of "speciesism." *See, e.g.,* Peter Singer, *Animal Liberation.*

only humans have the ability of empathetic communication.[39] That is, the political Left abruptly stops at the watershed of human communicative rationality.

People have the ability to share their experiences, to induce intellectual empathy from their fellows regarding the empirical. To the Left, this unique communicative ability in the species points to human uniqueness and to human equality. Yet, in the final analysis, *this privileging of human communicative ability—but refusing to privilege anything else—is nothing other than a Value Judgment.* Mandating the set behind the Veil of Ignorance as the whole of the human species, no more no less, could be described as Liberalism's one free miracle, damning the whole experiment as justifying nothing.

That Popper's Open Society also presents an exercise in question-begging, again necessarily condemns this project in the eyes of the Right. It simply presumes the grounds of debate by

---

39 *See* Jurgen Habermas, *The Theory of Communicative Action.*

unilaterally defining the meaning of "rational argument" in a self-serving way. And "heads I win, tails you lose," is a game in which no sane man engages. Thus, the Left's unselfconscious demand for universal tolerance is flagrantly absurd. It points up not only a paradox, but an impenetrable one as well.

Proponents of the Open Society demand that any actor be able to rationally argue, to justify, his actions to those potentially holding a different worldview, *i.e.*, he must uphold universal tolerance. Only those practicing universal tolerance qualify as rational actors. Again, Karl Popper:

> [A]s long as we can counter them by **rational argument** and keep them in check by public opinion, suppression would certainly be unwise. But we should claim the right to suppress them if necessary even by force; for it may easily turn out that **they are not prepared to meet us** on the level of **rational argument**, but begin by denouncing all argument...[40]

---

40 Karl Popper, *The Open Society and its Enemies*.

Yet, contrary to the claims of the Left, "intolerant philosophies" do not eschew all argument. The "intolerant" only claim the right to oppose differing societal circumstances from the level of rational argument ***intrinsic to those philosophies***. Which is not different in nature from what Karl Popper claims for his "tolerant philosophy." The nationalist treats the foreigner pursuant to the former's perceived duty to the nation. He must be able to justify his actions with respect to the principles of his nationalism. The Christian treats the non-Christian pursuant to the lights of Christianity. Presumably he must justify his actions to God.

At this point it becomes obvious that the concept of Reason is fundamentally different between Left and Right. For the Right, Reason serves to determine what Man is, and what he should do, not to dispassionately observe a chain of events and phenomena. Reason understood only as a process, grounded in nothing, purposeless, starting from nowhere and ultimately going nowhere, is nothing to the Right. Under such a scheme, even while

Man's "Reason" becomes an ever more powerful tool in service of material gratification—just as fangs evolve in the predator—it has no place in the service of Man as the person.

The Right obviously objects to the elevation of empiricism and materialism to the level of a religious confession. That the Left suggests a solution to the epistemological dispute in that both sides should come to an agreement upon a common belief in the inviolability of empirical, materialistic truths, while agreeing to disagree on everything else as unknowable, the Right calls this solution illusory. The problem with this resolution is that the empirical divorced from the non-empirical/speculative is something entirely different from the two ways of "knowing" co-joined into one seamless Truth. Endorsing empiricism by itself would be akin to mistaking a corpse for the body of a living person.

In the final analysis, one cannot engage in argument where the two sides have different understandings of the terms. If the two sides do not agree as to what constitutes evidence, or as to what constitutes rationality, their dialogue will be fruitless. Power (even if only at the ballot box) ends as the only arbiter. Ironically, this is the very tool Karl Popper would seem to eschew but quite evidently does not.

So to return to the paradox of universalism, if promoting tolerance pertained simply to the observation that, normatively-speaking, unthreatened people interact with each other tolerantly; then it would be merely to note a truism, grounded on description and perceived behavior, without need of further justification. But an observation of normative behavior is not a mandate without the addition of something more. To aim substantively, to claim that dialogue using tolerance-based language and terms are required, because the Open Society is self-evidently a superior mode of life; this amounts to a solipsism, and a juvenile one at that. Self-evident is the one thing that it is not. It does not take much to recognize that a mandate for universal tolerance collapses into ***nothing more than the Liberal's own preference***. It is tolerance only for those who prefer to live as the tolerant do, with No Society. Put in more practical terms, Left multiculturalism does not make the world safe for multiple cultures, but threatens all of them equally, making cessation of culture the inexorable result. Rather than freeing them, the "Open Society" condemns men to live within themselves.

That is, setting aside the myriad and profound problems of working this out in context, succinctly-put, the systemization of mandated tolerance must end in one unquestionable dogma: The individual human and his material needs are the measure of all things, and no other personal conclusions can be tolerated. As this dogma is further premised upon a teleology-free universe, the Right calls this dogma nonsense. Those on the Right cannot accept this dogma for themselves—liberal ideals are not the default aspirations of Humanity.[41] For the Right, compelled conformity regarding inclusiveness is both

---

[41] Notably, this points up another irony: While the Right can tolerate the existence of those who do not share its mode of life, the Left cannot do this. Illiberal Liberalism?

perplexing and oxymoronic—demanding it dialogue with the Left while the Left only talks to itself, thereby caving in the entire system—and inducing the Right to disengage and simply act.

Therefore, the Tolerance Paradox remains a paradox. While Liberalism maintains that intolerance and a Closed Society are only manifestations of irrational fear, this ignores the very real possibility that for many on the Right some kind of "Closed Society" is not a means of hysterically protecting themselves, but, in effect, an end unto itself. The practical manifestation of the current Liberal penchant for mandated tolerance translates into insisting that citizens effectively not hold preferences for the societies in which they live, or at least not act upon such preferences.

The current debate on American and Canadian university campuses regarding free speech is perhaps a good example of the working out of the Left's problem with tolerance, and the Right's reaction thereto. Given the current climate that sees the Left enforcing speech codes and "political correctness," it would be easy to dismiss the Left's position as simple hypocrisy of the first order, and some on the Right do just this. This would be a simplistic conclusion however. For the Left, free speech is a shibboleth. Notably this shibboleth results not from the belief that free speech is the best mechanism to discover the truth—as there is no truth to discover—but because you have the right to say anything . . . so long as your speech does not harm anyone else. And harm is to be gauged from the perspective of the Open Society.

In reality, the practical explanation and resolution for Left censorship today lies in fear. Speech codes on campuses, whether enforced formally or informally, are a result of Leftist fears that someone will be **persuaded** by illiberal speech, to seek illiberal, Closed Society results. As such, the Left does not threaten the freedom to speak; *it threatens the freedom of others to hear.*

While the Left can and does cite to certain kinds of hate speech as a form of verbal assault, it is far more concerned with the possibility that others will be persuaded to turn from, or awakened to, the disagreeable ramifications of liberal values. If Leftists protest the presence of certain speakers on college campuses, it is because they fear that the "innocent" listeners may find the speakers' words galvanizing, or at least thought provoking. Potentially threatening openness, inclusiveness, universality.

Perhaps it might be said that the Left pursues less a utopia, than the universality of a utopian worldview. This would explain an additional dogma for the Left—the purported demand for absolute separation of Church and State (regardless of what the community as a whole should believe, or wish[42]).

The Right retorts that this separation of Church and State is something of a façade, if viewed from a different perspective. While a church institution and a recognized state may be separated structurally, whether the state could ever be separated from a church in more

---

42 Because there is no real community of the whole. There are only associations of individuals.

essential terms begs many questions, most obviously and fundamentally, what exactly is meant by the terms "church" and "state"? To the point, the purported separation is in truth more directed today in separating the state from religion, rather than from any kind of institutional structure. Herein lies the rub.

If religion is rightly understood as a belief held in common within a community, to include a view as to the perceived reality encompassing the community as well as the ends of persons and of communal existence—that these in fact *are religio*—the Left has no intention of separating the state from religion. Furthermore, if religion pertains to finding Man's purpose, and the state pertains to supporting this with material means—in the case of the liberal state, the state exists to support each individual's purpose in engendering self-actualization—it becomes obvious that the goal of separation of state and religion would be a Quixotic aim. In reality all states are confessional, including liberal democratic ones, and all true religions are by definition, civic. It makes perfect sense then to expect all citizens in a liberal society to celebrate Bastille Day or Martin Luther King Day, although Christmas and Ramadan would be entirely private affairs. The entire campaign of the Left is a religious project.

The Left's auto-destructive paradoxes continue, in the Right's view. Particularly given that Progress in the Left's lexicon carries a meaning that is almost the antithesis of what it means for the Right, the Left anathematizes the latter's March of History. For the Right, going from, say, Neolithic Man to modern Man is part of the positive March of History. Yet this march required an infinite number of oft-imposed sacrifices along the way, intrinsically causing angst for the Left. And certainly the Left is loath to value modern civilization as qualitatively superior in any moral sense over "primitive" existence.

As such, addressing history is extremely problematical for the Left, at least without the application of transformative anachronism *i.e.*, the past is simply an unfolding of the present.[43] Indeed, in some sense the Left has a future but no past because, even in tracing its own course, the Left inevitably disavows that past as insufficiently liberated.

Yet, how to criticize, when one's ground and ability for criticism are the fruit of those very impositions that are part and parcel of the March of History? To cite one specific example is Feminism. Given that only in recent centuries has infant mortality dropped to levels sustainable for a human existence with a low level of reproduction, how can Feminism unreservedly criticize the historical "subjugation" of women? Without the life paths of women in the distant past steered at least to some degree toward submission, a sexual role, child-rearing, and domestic concerns, there would be no modern Humanity to criticize this subjugation. The fact is that the Left's characterization of past life lived under something akin to Rightist

---

43 The Whiggish view of history is perhaps an apotheosis of such an application. *See, e.g.*, Lord Macaulay, *The History of England*.

principles as representing an immiserating form of existence, discounts the reality that these Rightist principles in some measure made life possible.

Additionally, it is no secret that the Left objects to the fact that respect for the past impedes the freedom of the present. Past generations impose themselves upon present and future generations via the "dead hand of history."

The problem is that the logic of the dead hand, if not the dead hand itself, necessarily includes the future as well as the past. Future generations are a "burden" on the present. The present is forced to consider the future, in terms of both resource management and ecological sustainability, as well as continued social cohesion. The present is forced to budget, sacrifice, and to some extent, conform. At the very least, a community's offspring require investment in terms of their rearing and provisioning. All are called upon to contribute communally, directly or indirectly, regardless of whether one has, or even wants to have, children. These children constitute the next generation of workers, defenders, and the very continuation of the community.

As a practical matter drawn from the headlines of today, the immigration debate illustrates how the Left in the West addresses this, at least in the short term, and how egalitarian principles nicely mate up with the solution. The problem of the need for social security and for the continuity of the community without burdening the present with babies can be short-circuited by simply importing fully formed persons, *i.e.*, immigrants. The community is benefited without having to put forward the outlay. The dead hand of history is severed. The only things that suffer are blood ties, which are a null value for the Left in moral terms.[44] Thus, consumerism and liberating birth control can be encouraged, and immigrants make up labor shortfalls and provide continuation for the community into the future.

---

44 Indeed, giving birth to children may be the greatest of discriminatory and "racist" actions one can take under this logic.

The Right dismisses the logic of the dead hand of history altogether. To it, for the Left to resort to the problem of the future of the community with the—it must be admitted—only very short-term solution of immigration; this only demonstrates the poverty of the Leftist moral imagination. It is as if—to borrow a concept from Bertold Brecht—the government was looking to elect a new people. The Leftist solution proposes that some communities consume themselves for the pleasures of the day, while other communities effectively serve as organ-donors. This may be one reason why Pope John Paul II suggested the modern West to be a civilization slipping into a "culture of death."

Yet, today, it is perhaps most of all in the practice of politics that the conflict between Left and Right becomes most glaring and threatens a decisive breach between the two sides. For the Left the very word "democracy" has content. It does not simply name a particular mechanistic means for arriving at political decisions, the mere instrumentality of voting and holding elections. Leftist democracy is an ethical ideal rather than a political arrangement. For democracy to be authentically democratic, it must affirm liberal principles. That is both its justification and its reason for being. If its exercise results in an illiberal outcome, this is not really legitimate democracy. It is not entitled to respect in such an event, notwithstanding the inviolable esteem afforded democracy by the Left otherwise. Where an electorate exercises choice to choose something other than advancing an inclusive and indeterminate openness, where it defies universalism, and bases its decisions in respect of religion, rank, or race for instance; the Left calls itself justified in defying this so-called "democracy" in turn.

In contrast, despite some healthy room for circumspection, typically for the Right democracy means just what it is commonly understood to mean: It is simply a form of governance, one where all the members of a posited whole have a theoretically equal voice in the government of the whole. Any result can come of it, and democracy is simply a way of resolving political questions. There are no questions intrinsically off limits for it, at least not per the limits of the definition. That is, while there may be "fundamental rights" placed out of its bounds, *e.g.*, to "life, liberty, and property," these rights are understood to be accretions, even if prized and necessary, to democracy in itself. If the rules of democracy are followed, the results are by definition democratic.

Not so for the Left. For the Enlightenment Left every *homo sapiens* is intrinsically entitled to inclusion and to that transcendent concept called "human rights," without regard to the ballot box. While today's Left has difficulty identifying the exact substance of these human rights, and even more difficulty in divining their root; it has identified one procedural attribute of human rights: The Left asserts that any identity-based difference made between persons must be seen fundamentally as a corruption (*i.e.*, operating without a veil). Avoiding this corruption is the *sine qua non* for liberal democracy. Whether the difference is "imagined," such as race; or "natural," such as strength and intelligence, or place of birth, these are all "accidental" attributes threatening the dignity of Man. Man is One.

Perhaps indirectly derived from Immanuel Kant, or perhaps deriving further back from a particularly caustic form of neo-Platonic metaphysics, this attitude discovers Truth only in the horizon offered by an abstract, enlightened unity, *i.e.*, again, a kind of Monism. It denounces particularized reality as flawed, or in fact unreal. Gender, ethnicity, rank, historical context, even familial connections, these are all seen inevitably as some degree of corruption from a primordial human singularity.

For the Right, this attitude implicitly represents not only a political and ethical wrong, but also a metaphysical error. An erroneous view of being. It is for this reason that many on today's conservative Right are attached to the analogy to the movie *The Matrix*, which presents a Manichean plot wherein unconscious Humanity is connected to an unreal, materialistic world apparently of its subjects' own choosing. Much is felt, but nothing is real. Those who desire reality have to take "the red pill."

The Right asserts that actual life is a synthesis. Man is real, and Man is many. Human rights, duties, are necessarily relational, implying the precedence of felt (*i.e.*, non-empirically-grounded) solidarity, society, and order. Loyalty. There is no equality. There are no innate human rights.

There are no "rights" vis-à-vis Nature. What right to life, liberty, and property is there, in the face of want, or in the face of a hurricane? Or in the face of a pack of wolves?[45] A human right held by one person self-evidently must correspond to a duty held by another person or persons. And there is no duty imposed in a vacuum.[46]

---

45 *See* Yuval Noah Harari, *A Brief History of Humankind.*

46 To quote Comte Joseph de Maistre, who, along with Edmund Burke, is one of the two founders of modern political Conservatism: "Now, there is no such thing as 'man' in this world. In the course of my life, I have seen Frenchmen, Italians, Russians, etc. . . . But, as for Man, I declare that I have never met him in my life. If he exists, I certainly have no

Thus, Rousseau asked the wrong questions. The questions are not: What right does one person have to compel another? What right does one person have to exclude another? Rather, the real questions are: What right does one have to inclusion, to freedom from compulsion? That is, what duty does a person have to forswear exclusion, or to foreswear command? From whence do these duties arise? The only answer is that they arise from the engendering of ever-increasing spheres of identity.

As such, in the Right's view *contra* Rousseau, ordered society, even slavery, is not the continuation of Hobbes's war of all against all, **but its cessation**. Civilization interdicts universal, perpetual competition and conflict— this state of conflict being the theoretical, pre-societal and egalitarian human condition postulated by the Left.[47] The bonds of feeling,

---

knowledge of him." *Considerations sur la France.*

47 Although Hobbesianism is often ascribed to the Right, it is worth noting that it is at root a perspective of contractarianism, and, as such, of the Left. The "State of Nature" sees Man in his core essence, as individual, naturally free and

belief, and loyalty interdict animalism. In sum, while prophets may indeed have revealed the rights of men to the world, such rights are normatively prescribed by history, consensus . . . perhaps even by democracy . . . but not by a groundless, pointless, and ironically irrational, self-referential "Reason."

---

unmoored in any society, a *tabula rasa*. In fact Liberalism has by its own admission advanced a convenient fiction in this concept, a "State of Nature." As Sir Robert Filmer characterized it in *Patriarcha*, pre-societal Man is only a glib postulate of puerile thinking, which no one can claim to be historical.

CONCLUSION

To sum up, the Right makes choices, takes objective positions. The Left reacts to rebut those choices as ill-founded and, furthermore, unjustifiable, and points to what a just society would look like in their absence. The Right remains unconvinced by the attempted rebuttal, and even questions the pertinence of requiring justification for the most fundamental of its evaluations. Moreover, in the Right's view the Left's default position also constitutes a choice—but one that the Left in turn refuses to justify, denying that it constitutes such a choice. Unless those on the Right can be pried from their many evaluations, *e.g.*, that identity is superior to a *tabula rasa*, that civilization is superior to its absence, that some cultures are subjectively preferable to others, the existence of a Right will continue to be innate. To this extent it seems that the conflict between the Left and Right is intractable, with ominous potential ramifications.

Given the refusal by the Left to analyze what itself deems self-evident, and given the Left's recent dominance, it sometimes seems that the meta-politics of the institutions governing today's Western society—from parliaments and universities, to the press and the law guilds—are oriented primarily to ensuring that those who do not affirmatively profess a universalist and materialist religion cannot engage, or even survive. The Right is routinely condemned by those institutions ***not in how it conducts itself, but in what it desires, and in what it values***. Thus, the Right has an uphill battle in the public square, as the Overton Window has seemingly been configured specifically to exclude it from participation.

It is hard to deny that some kind of disloyalty seems to be a requirement to have standing with regard to politics, and particularly with regard to the academy. Disloyalty to one's European identity for instance. Disloyalty to the traditions, hierarchy, and faith of the West. Jettisoning these identities appear to be the *sine qua non* for publicly acceptable discourse. In the institutions of the academy, a Leftist position can be labelled "extremist," insofar as it appeals to extreme means, *e.g.*, the 1793 Reign of Terror. In contrast, the Right can be labeled extreme, even if its actors are as peaceful as Gandhi, if it strays into the waters of Western particularism. What the Right wants, values, or loves is damnable—not just what the Right does. Moreover, in terms of more practical constitutional and existential questions of nation-states, instead of inviting peaceful Right-wing contribution in the public forum, it appears from the viewpoint of the average Conservative that the political establishment is almost daring him to extra-legal action.

Of course, the Right is hardly alone in accusing the dominant paradigm in Western liberal democracy of engendering a civilization-wide political establishment that refuses to represent all its constituency as such. The radical Left, for one, has been decrying this situation for years. But, the Right's "National Front"-position is unique in the extent of its current political disenfranchisement.

The Right today obviously aims to alter this circumstance, and its aim is ultimately civilization-wide. Nonetheless, its first level of engagement is undoubtedly the nation (nation-state?). As such, today's Right indeed holds some of the same famous (infamous?) attitudes taken up by the intellectuals of the Conservative Revolution in Germany in the 1920s, and by the National Fronts of Spain and France in the 1930s.

This is only to say that the chasm between the Left and Right is truly profound. The two sides do not disagree as to the procedures of communal life, as much as they disagree on the very purposes of community and of governance. Again, they disagree not so much about means, as ends. One side sees the state and governance as vehicles to promote universal, liberal principles, or at least to serve as shields to defend those principles, *i.e.*, to prevent the Right from getting what it wants.

The other side sees living, "irrational" Man himself as the purpose of the state. As such, the latter sees government's purpose as doing what the tribe, the community, or the "nation" (in however way the nation is constituted, and expresses itself) wants done.

The Right today dares to ask, what is a nation? The simplest, unquestionable definition to this question is of course that a nation is an imagined community.[48] But for the Right, imagination starts at birth. With blood. Which implies family and traditions, with all their inherited orders. And it implies ethnicity. He who denies his ethnic identity may as well deny his family as well, because he would be no more justified in elevating family in rational terms than ethnicity.

In contrast, the Left-rational man appears to deny that men are born as particular men; rather, they are born as abstract souls without bodies (or perhaps it is bodies without souls, depending upon where one finds the

---

48 *See* Ernest Renan, *Qu'est-ce qu'une nation?*; Benedict Anderson, *Imagined Communities*.

particularities of the actual human person). He affirms T. S. Eliot's hollow men. So, the Right's political project, if there is one, aims to affirm in the face of the Left, the whole person— including Race, Rank, and Religion—and to dissolve the false consciousness of a materialist, *homo economicus.*[49]

To be clear, neither the Left nor the Right endorses nihilism or chaos. Both endorse "Value" as the proper end of Humanity. Indeed, after a fashion, the Left may be said to be as devoted to the Good, the Beautiful, and the True, as its opponent. But the Left in effect proposes that humans not aim at Value immediately or directly, and certainly not in any kind of communal sense. Rather, Humanity should first work for a world where everyone can find, or create, his or her own personal Value. In contrast, the Rights says Value, the Good, the Beautiful, and the True, should be pursued now, immediately. Do the right thing. Disengage yourself from a fruitless

---

49 *See* Hannah Arendt, *The Human Condition.*

dialogue and make a choice. This may mean taking others into equal consideration, when doing the right thing. Or it may not.[50]

So, while the Left is fighting to remove what it deems to be mere "preference" as the basis for human intercourse, the Right is fighting for those very preferences. In the Right's view, the Left appears to be fighting for nothing and nothingness. In contrast, as no one disputes, people on the Right are fighting, frankly, for themselves.

The Left and Right are still fighting in the cultural and religious realms. The Left has however, dominated the political, legal, journalistic, and educational realms of the West for many decades. At least until now.

In the final analysis, while the two sides are indeed opponents, they are not mirror images of one another. The political Left aims at an ideal law for an ideal polity, at least to

---

50 The Right contends that no Pyramid, Cathedral, or Ferrari would have ever been built, no new worlds ever discovered; if the material interests of all had been taken into equal consideration, as the Left demands.

the extent that law and governance can bring about this state of affairs. That is, the Left is oriented toward a particular state of political and social being—a world order of prosperous self-actualization, utopia—even if ever over the horizon.[51]

The other side, as a meta-political project, does not aim at a utopia of self-actualization, or any kind of utopia at all. At root, the Right does not aim for an ideal polity, but at a new beginning for a re-established "real" polis, one where political life exists to make real choices, evaluations. Practically-speaking, the Right is first oriented around building a secure political space for the recognition of "particular peoples, in particular places."[52] It is for this reason that

---

51 Ironically, some on the Left seem to concede that its project is impossible in practical terms, self-abnegating, inasmuch as the fulfillment of one concrete goal only leads to the formulation of another. Obtaining the ability ***to get what one wants*** does not simultaneously bequeath the ability ***to determine what one wants***, and may in fact detract from this latter ability.

52 As an aside here at the end, the very political establishment in the West seems to view many of its institutions, including property as well as national territory, as a kind theft

the Right is fighting for its assumptions, its preferences.

Most fundamentally, the Right seems ultimately oriented around establishing the premises whereat real politics—in pursuit of the Good, the Beautiful, and the True, as those who make up the Right understand these concepts—could actually begin again. After all, a hierarchical, differentiated, but relatively homogeneous society is ***not an end but a beginning***. The Right is thus oriented toward the place from whence to start the journey to the Undiscovered Country of the Good, the Beautiful, and the True, which is a place beyond politics.

---

unless tied to need. There is no right to exclude, only a normative duty to include, based upon perceived need. This is not the view of the Right.